Ho

Every Year

John Lowe

A Lowe Publication™

Text © John Lowe, 2011.

The right of John Lowe to be identified as author of this work has been asserted by him in accordance with the Copyright, Designs and Patents Act 1988.

All rights reserved. No part of this publication may be reproduced or transmitted in any form or by any means, electronic or mechanical, including photocopy, recording or any information storage and retrieval system, without permission in writing from the publisher.

Published in 2011 by:

**Lowe Publications
Linen Hall, 162 Regent Street
London, W1B 5TG
United Kingdom**

ISBN: 978-1-907824-08-1

Layout and illustrations by Giorgio Giussani.

Edited by Judi Hunter.

Printed in London by Empress Litho Ltd.

How to Have a Gap Year *Every* Year *challenges the boring tramline thinking regarding career ladders and encourages the reader to 'stand back' and review all their exciting options.*

It empowers you to apply your skills to an activity that you enjoy, which does not involve the overplayed transformational or transactional leader moulds or having to use big sentences that must contain hackneyed jargon like 'global strategy', 'return on investment', 'search engine optimisation', 'planning tools', or 'quantitative and qualitative analysis'.

Throw off the shackles of corporate role playing – you are the boss. Have your own board meeting – you are the new MD.

Contents

About the author	**8**
Introduction	**10**
Is it a personality thing?	
Does personality matter?	**12**
Personality type – which am I?	**14**
The Supporter	15
Descriptive lexicon	17
The Supporter and their interactions	17
The Influencer	19
Descriptive lexicon	20
The Influencer and their interactions	21
The Creative	24
Descriptive lexicon	25
The Creative and their interactions	25
The Analyst	27
Descriptive lexicon	28
The Analyst and their interactions	28

The coach trip of personalities — 30
- The Supporter's choice — 32
- The Influencer's choice — 33
- The Creative's choice — 33
- The Analyst's choice — 34

Work is changing — 36
- The good old days — 37
- The good new days — 39

Can work be play? — 40

Which factors motivate people to review career options? — 44
- Is it an age thing? — 45
- Is it an opt out or a cop out? — 46
- Should you plan it or just go for it? — 47

Let's round up — 52

About the author

John Lowe, founding director of Regent Selection, Regent Coaching and Regent eLearning, is the author of *Your Lowe Profile* and one of the leading experts on career and personal development coaching.

John is a successful headhunter, recruitment consultant and coach and it is this rare combination of skills and his experience of having conducted over 20,000 interviews – all factors which collectively give him unique market and people insight. He personally coaches MBA students, university professors, Board directors and an extensive range of business executives.

The coaching always has a strong employability focus and John's first-hand knowledge of the market place is based on his expertise of conducting assignments with the world's largest corporations, SMEs and start-ups. Each industry and employment activity has its own dynamic and the structure and content of the coaching has been designed to embrace this divergence and variety. John has introduced an exciting new approach to conventional coaching through the identification and development of four distinct personality types. As the candidate recognises their type and individual strengths, they can then apply this knowledge to the critical employment stages of knowing what is their ideal job role, always successfully performing on interview and consistently enhancing a top performance at work. All these critical factors are described in the publication *Your Lowe Profile*, which can be used as an expert career coaching reference.

On a personal note John is a graduate of the University of London where his Masters in Philosophy had a particularly contemporary focus on the role of ethics in our changing workplace.

Introduction

I don't think the idea of having a gap year for one year, or even every year, is going to be a sudden revelation, a sudden out-of-body experience. It is more likely to be something you have been thinking about and 'had in the back of your mind' for some time. Perhaps this booklet may give you the conviction to turn your idea into a reality.

I am deliberately using a discursive style so as to engage with you, the reader, as though we are in dialogue together. In this booklet, I will address issues that, in my experience, highlight the most common concerns and challenges for people wishing to break the typical career mould.

I have always encouraged people to be ambitious in their thinking and have gained a lot of personal satisfaction from being the facilitator to help many achieve their 'dream'.

When you have read this booklet and still feel positive

about your plan, your goal, your idea – then just do it. Even the preparation stage can act as a catalyst in terms of finding out how motivated you are. I have known several people to change their minds while planning new ventures. This change indicated that, while they were still seeking a career change, their particular choice was not right either from a time or logistical perspective.

If you love the idea of having a gap year every year, then you will also enjoy reading this booklet. It takes an unconventional approach to traditional norms. It undermines the rule that a structured career path is for everyone and it challenges ambition, performance, achievement, industry growth and promotion as being suppositional establishment terms and not necessarily the only aspirational life goal setters.

This booklet is written in sympathy with the above theme and is deliberately not structured, since to consider having a gap year every year would require breaking with convention in our approach to would-be norms.

Is it a personality thing? Does personality matter?

Your personality is important when considering a gap year because your perspective on situations will depend on it. Certain personality types will be highly adventurous, enjoy taking risks or aiming for dramatic lifestyle changes. Other types will be more cautious and endeavour to negotiate the 'parachute option' with their employer – they will request a sabbatical, knowing that their job is secure when they return to work.

If you are considering having a gap year, you should first endeavour to ascertain your personality type and then match it to your strengths and interests. Your personality will influence your choice of activity and what you gain in terms of experience from that activity. We are aware of the maxim that travel broadens the mind, but that is not always the case. We know of narrow-minded adventurers who view new experiences from a narrow perspective and can return from their travels with an even more insular and intolerant attitude.

Personality type – which am I?

When the chosen activity is a good fit you will enjoy it, feel motivated and happy. It is therefore highly beneficial to identify your particular personality type. Reviewing your past in terms of the activities you enjoyed and disliked is a very good benchmark when you are reviewing the personality descriptors.

But how do you find out your personality type? Perhaps a session with an expert psychologist or, if not that, there must be a questionnaire to fill out which can be processed by a computer and 'eureka' you have a report?

Think: who really knows you best? Who is the person who has noted all your successes, mistakes, funny quirks, good and bad moods, happy and sad times and, despite all the different reactions and situations, can make sense of the different behaviours and contradictions and find a very well-defined personality type? You know this person well…

You are your own best judge. From my experience of coaching, candidates have related very positively to the process I use of outlining scenarios whereby they can contextually make sense of their previous actions and decisions. Understanding yourself will ensure that the activity you undertake is sustainable and enjoyable.

Knowing yourself better means that you can choose better.

Knowing yourself better means that you know what you are good at.

Knowing others better means that you can be more tolerant and judge others in the context of their intention, rather than in the context of their actions.

Review the following personality descriptors and identify the type that most clearly relates to you. It is important to know.

The Supporter

In common parlance, the Supporter could be described as a 'people person'. They are good judges of character and have a strong ability to empathise with others.

In terms of the corporate environment, the Supporter likes to display the following characteristics:

- Enjoys helping people and gaining recognition for doing so.
- Engages with colleagues on a meaningful and personal basis.
- Will support weaker members of a team and help them to develop.
- Empathetic and sensitive to others – strong aptitude for customer care and client services.
- Dislikes confrontation and does not voluntarily interact with truculent, domineering types.
- A tendency to be over concerned regarding the sensitivities of colleagues and to lose focus in terms of commercial objectives.

The strong people aspect of their personality will mean that their judgements and comments will be from the people perspective. Their descriptions will focus on the players rather than the game, the actors rather than the film, the personnel rather than the project.

Descriptive lexicon

Trainer	Caring	Intuitive
Good communicator	Instructor	Good listener
Adaptable	Compliant	Coach
Co-operative	Compassionate	Collaborative
Mentor	Patient	Team player
Conformist	Sympathetic	Tolerant
Trustworthy	Positive	Friendly
Honest	Reliable	Unselfish
Empathetic	Sensitive	Thoughtful
Sincere	Flexible	Stable

The Supporter and their interactions

The Supporter views situations from the people perspective. They are good judges of character and will understand and empathise with people's strengths, weaknesses, concerns and problems. They will be influenced by people's mood. If their friends are happy, they will want to join them and share their joy or good news.

Supporters are good team builders. They can choose different types to complement a working environment. They 'get on well' together. They 'like' each other. Their comments about people will be emotionally based. Supporters are sensitive and do not like truculent aggressive types whom they will avoid, interacting only when necessary.

In the commercial environment, Supporters need to constantly modify and reaffirm their focus to see their duties and responsibilities in a task and goal oriented form, rather than based predominately on 'people interactions' with obscurely defined commercial objectives.

Supporters are moody and enjoy sharing their feelings with others. They are loyal, reliable and honest and will not voluntarily interact with people who are unreliable, dishonest and, in their mind, lacking the most fundamental characteristic if they are to be their friend – integrity.

It is important that the Supporter feels valued by their employer. Recognition for good effort will ensure that the Supporter is highly motivated and committed. Trust is one of the Supporter's highest values. If you are a friend, they will expect that trust to be reciprocated. If you break that trust, the Supporter may ostracise you as a friend and you will have difficulty regaining that confidence.

The Influencer

The Influencer is articulate and outgoing and may be described as being 'a good talker'. They are likely to display the following qualities:

- Outgoing and talkative.
- Enjoys the social aspect of the work environment. Has a wide circle of friends and dislikes 'sitting in'.
- Always shares their opinions and experiences with others.
- A good leader whom others find inspirational.
- A strong negotiator and sales person.
- Likely to dominate group meetings.
- Highly political in a work environment.

An Influencer has good commercial acumen and can be motivated by the prospect of earning commission or a bonus based on performance. They will endeavour to take up promotion opportunities and, consequently, can move up the career ladder faster. A higher income also gives them the option to indulge in 'good taste' for expensive purchases.

Descriptive lexicon

Lively	Resourceful	Positive
Commercially aware	Engaging	Motivational
Strong communicator	Decisive	Articulate
Competitive	Poor listener	Target driven
Fun	Vigorous	Witty
Results orientated	Challenging	Energetic
Convincing	Sociable	Inspiring
Spontaneous	Adventurous	Believable

The Influencer and their interactions

The Influencer, like the Supporter, has a predominant people orientation. They enjoy people interaction but will have less people empathy than a Supporter. They may manifest an introvert or an extrovert personality. They have a propensity to adjust their behaviour to suit the situation.

The Influencer is extremely flexible and adaptable and will endeavour to establish a positive rapport with their manager. They recognise corporate hierarchy and can be relied on to get a job done. Their positive mindset/ego is their driver.

If they produce a great performance, the Influencer expects a great response: 'You were great.' 'That's the best!' 'Congratulations!' 'How did you do that?' 'Oh, it was nothing,' is their polite response as they gloat in the adulation. The Influencer has a positive disposition and is a good talker. The natural flipside to being a good talker is being a poor listener.

'Let me tell you about the bargain I got on eBay. Can anyone guess how much I paid for these?' Whether anyone is interested in the items, their value or how much the Influencer paid are not factors that would be remotely considered by the Influencer. If challenged conversationally, they will sternly defend their position.

The Influencer's large ego does not allow much room for modesty. Their predominant work pattern is to perform and manage through verbal influence. If colleagues are reluctant to co-operate, the Influencer will engage verbally and 'sell' the idea.

Influencers are strong time managers but poor at assimilating detail. 'It's the big picture that counts,' will be their energetic philosophy. Identifying the core facts can be a challenge to the Influencer, as the premise of 'how I say it' can be more persuasive than 'what I say'.

A striking presentation may have to sacrifice content and detail and, therefore, the Influencer may apply embellishment and exaggeration to persuade the audience. This is acceptable behaviour from their perspective, providing the audience is not misled and the substance is true.

They are self-centred and enjoy sharing their ideas. They enjoy lively debate and challenging other opinions, raising the tempo by expressing controversial and non-conformist viewpoints. Influencers are likeable, positive, active, have a good sense of humour and a 'can do' mentality.

The Influencer may become lazy if their work does not motivate them. They are easily bored and will move jobs more often than most. Money, variety and challenge are their drivers and they will aim to achieve targets and receive commission. Their vocabulary is often supercharged with emotive terms.

'Life and soul of the party' is a good description and whether at a party or at work the Influencer will be very interested in what people do. Status is important to the Influencer.

The Creative

The Creative is a lateral Analyst with the ability to think 'outside the square' and bring a fresh, original perspective to workplace challenges. The following characteristics are typical of the Creative:

- A creative aptitude, which can manifest as a special design talent or a strong appreciation of the arts.
- Takes nothing for granted.
- Enjoys new ideas and non-traditional routes to problem solving.
- Confidently states opinions on advertising campaigns, market trends and future product and lifestyle developments.
- Over sensitive at times and does not take criticism well.
- Has difficulties with time management and works on the philosophy of 'Give me more time and I can do an even better job.'
- Has 3D visualisation.

Descriptive lexicon

Interesting	Adventurous	Expressive
Pioneering	Unconventional	Visualiser
Industrious	Creative	Conscentious
Demanding	Analytical	Designer
Optimistic	Efficient	A 'can do' attitude
Conceptual	Talented	Deliberate
Organised	Judgemental	Good listener

The Creative and their interactions

The Creative has an amazing ability to visualise conceptually from many perspectives. They create designs relating to architecture, products, fashion and packaging; write books, plays, lyrics, advertising jingles; paint, illustrate; compose, perform, etc. – creations that have underpinned the worldwide success of some of our best-known products, art, architecture, music, advertising and fashion.

The Creative can be opinionated and stubborn and will generally defend any criticism of their work.

When I am describing personality types, I am predominantly describing the trait or characters in isolation and outlining the main or predominant behaviours for that particular type. Picasso, Yehudi Menuhin, and Andrew Lloyd-Webber manifest unique creative talents.

The Creative has a talent that they must have the scope to manifest or apply. The architect must design. The artist must paint. The Creative has a strong talent for design and they are motivated when they are positively developing and applying that talent within a practical application.

The Creative is open and transparent in their views and will enjoy intellectualising discussions.

The Analyst

The prevailing quality of the Analyst is the ability to approach and solve problems in a highly rational, structured manner. In terms of personality characteristics, the following are likely to apply:

- Enjoys the challenge of working things out independently.
- Enjoys problem solving – the greater the problem, the greater the challenge and the greater the intellectual satisfaction.
- Happier expressing facts over feelings.
- Lacks motivation if the task in hand is perceived to be pointless.
- Enjoys their own company.
- A good listener.
- Lacking in verbal spontaneity.

Descriptive lexicon

Reliable	Consistent	Sceptical
Tolerant	Technical	Independent
Patient	Analytical	Thorough
Stable	Meticulous	Adaptable
Good listener	Deliberate	Thoughtful
Determined	Logical	Accurate
Problem solver	Resilient	Industrious

The Analyst and their interactions

The Analyst is clinical in their judgements. They are not predominately people oriented and have a clear focus on the task in hand. Interestingly, during past recessions, more Analysts have been seen to be new business starters though they are not natural entrepreneurs. Historically, this was the Influencer's home territory.

For example, technology, not people, present scope for the Analyst to develop a new software tool and launch it via the internet. There is no face-to-face people sales contact. Their clever technology may identify and satisfy a market gap and need. The technology is also a non-people platform on which to market and launch. They can be today's new entrepreneurs. Think of the founders of the world's largest and most successful IT companies.

The Analyst can be considered introverted. They are thoughtful in response, rarely circumlocutory and only comment on what they know. The Analyst does not hold grudges and, if offended, reviews the situation circumspectly rather than personally, commenting something along the lines of, 'They would say that, wouldn't they?'

Analysts are not good time managers. They can be too fastidious in their work mentality, and when applying themselves to a task can supply a level of detail that was neither prescribed nor required.

The coach trip of personalities

Some people like to plan, others enjoy spontaneity. Your approach will depend on your personality type. The Analyst will take a cautious, calculated approach. The Influencer will be cavalier, dealing with situations as they occur. The Supporter will look for activities that involve opportunities to mix with other groups. The Influencer, too, will enjoy the company of groups, but will seek only those groups within which they would be recognised for their achievements and be given elevated status. The Analyst will be happy studying rock formation in some remote mountainous region. The Creative, similarly, will take pleasure in exploring the Seven Wonders of the World.

Imagine a coach trip to the site of a well-known volcano. How would the perspective of the different personalities influence their experience of the visit?

The Supporter would spend the journey engaging with the other passengers and would judge the excursion in terms of how they related to the group: 'Great day. Met lots of new people.'

The Influencer would enjoy being the guide or the coach driver, or playing a role where they could perform and be recognised. Influencers may read up on the background information and would make sure that they share and impart this knowledge to the group to gain complimentary recognition.

The Creative would observe the volcano in its spatial context, its dimensions, colour, shape and backdrop. They might be fascinated by its visual impact and its majesty of relational proportionality.

The Analyst would be interested in reading the material concerning the history of the volcano, would be fascinated by observing it first hand and comparing the phenomena with the science.

Most people have a dominant and secondary trait and will judiciously and sublimely apply these selectively to situations. For example, if your dominant personality type is Analyst and your secondary trait is Supporter, you will diligently and exclusively apply your computational skills in the conduct of qualitative analysis and apply your Supporter skills whilst explaining the results and their implications to a non-technical audience.

The descriptors below relate the personality types to their approach to having a gap year.

The Supporter's choice

The Supporter is a people person and should choose an activity in which they can be part of a group. Unlike the Influencer, they do not have the need to lead or perform. They prefer to instruct and take a share in helping. Thus, the group activity should not be one of a highly competitive nature. The contention and disagreement that competition inevitably involves will cause the Supporter stress and they will not enjoy the experience, particularly when the parties involved adopt an irreconcilable attitude. If you are a Supporter, your activity should be non-competitive and reliant on a collaborative and collective approach. The Supporter is very sensitive and empathetic – core ingredients for a strong team player and motivator. The motto is: 'A happy team is a successful team.'

The Influencer's choice

The Influencer is good at selling, is outgoing, people-orientated and enjoys being 'the life and soul of the party'. Recognition and a platform to perform are important criteria. Thus, they will choose an activity that is high profile, challenging and one that has plenty of scope to demonstrate their achievements. The Influencer is big on people-interaction and enjoys the opportunity to encourage others to participate. They are good motivators, good to be with and prefer to see the cup half full rather than the negative connotation. They are strong people-persons who relish recognition and ego-enhancing activities.

The Creative's choice

The Creative should naturally choose an activity where they have scope to design, invent and create or where, if they are not the 'doers', they are the 'appreciators'. For example, if you are a Creative, you could be an oil paint artist or a curator of a museum specialising in oil paint artists. In the former case, you would produce the artistic work. In the latter, you would enjoy the environment of art appreciation and evaluation.

Whether it is man-made or natural art, the Creative has a huge spectrum of choice which will, of course, be influenced by their specialism, whether it is in painting, literature, music, architecture or design.

The Creative will enjoy the company of people with a similar propensity. They will need variety and change as they do not adjust well to repetitive activities and have a low boredom threshold.

The Analyst's choice

For the Analyst to enjoy having a gap year every year they should choose an activity that has primarily a non-people focus and dependency. Mindful that the Analyst has a strong propensity for science and technical information, they should choose adventures that are intellectually challenging.

The Analyst enjoys the company of people with similar interests where they can engage in purposeful debate.

Spontaneous small talk is not their forte. The Analyst is also happy in their own company and does not need the constant stimulus of people interaction. Their activity will need to have a transparent and defined objective if it is to be enjoyable and sustainable.

Work is changing

This booklet, *How to Have a Gap Year Every Year*, does not imply that I want to do nothing. It does not mean that I want to lie in bed all day, get up when I want, watch some TV, socialise with friends in the evening or aimlessly surf the net.

One of the numerous definitions of work describes it as a 'sustained physical or mental effort to achieve a result'. Gosh, the definition itself sounds like hard work! 'Sustained' – I must not give up. 'Result' – I am being monitored and measured. On this basis, work is something to which I might have an instant aversion. If a career means presenting me with the prospect of having to apply myself to what I consider to be boring, repetitive tasks as my main role or only option for the next 10, 20 or 30 years, then the future prospects are daunting.

However, enjoyment at work is allowed. The great news is that today's work environment offers many options. My role as a recruitment consultant and career coach has facilitated countless people in their quest to 'opt out' or pursue an interest as their prime source of income. If having a gap year means doing what I enjoy for a year, why can't I extend the enjoyment and do it every year?

There is a merging of the two extreme views of what is construed as work and what is 'not a real job'. Gone are the huge hierarchical structures within large corporations where one's life ambition was to get on the 'next rung' of the promotion ladder. Management structures have flattened; technology has replaced the administrators; globalisation has dramatically increased competition; long-term planning is long-term guesswork; people-centric organisations have become task-centric. The future is so fluid and unpredictable that 'the new' is the only real measure or focus.

The good old days

Jobs for life, promotional prospects, final salary pensions, bottomless training budgets are all now remnants of the past and often referred to as 'the good times' – when you had job security; when loyalty was practised and valued as a work virtue; when you could phone a company without call queuing and speak to a real person; when employers were treated as people and given good pensions, luncheon vouchers and sent on several training courses and given a gold watch to count the interminable minutes of their retirement in recognition of a loyal service.

Halcyon days? Not for a moment. Substitute 'loyalty' for 'self-interest', 'job security' for 'prison sentence' and think boring, repetitive work. Changing career was almost impossible and when I resigned from one of the world's largest banks after three years, the manager remarked, 'What about your pension?' – a comment which allayed any reservations I had about my decision. Corporate structures were hierarchical, fixed and predictable. Your manager dictated your career growth and, therefore, your attitude was subservient and accommodating if you relished promotion via a positive annual report.

So how does this transition influence me if I want to have a gap year every year? 'Very directly' is the answer.

The short-termism prevalent within the job market means that an employer has a predominant new focus. 'Have you got the soft and technical skills to do the job now?' is their only criteria. They are not intending to give you lifelong employment, as the markets are too unpredictable. The same attitude suits the modern employee who prefers short-term commitment and the greater opportunity for change, variety and new challenges.

The good new days

I interview many candidates in today's job market who are planning or who have made a dramatic career change, a decision that has been encouraged and facilitated by the present market phenomena. I can see a time when the differentiation between work perceived as a duty and/or as an enjoyable activity will evaporate, and viewing a gap year as an escape lane or as being 'let out' will be an archaic concept. We shall all be on a gap year and doing more or less, and for most of the time, what we want to do. Roll on the future…!

Can work be play?

Society constantly distinguishes between work and play. Yet, we can also challenge this stereotypical view. Is there always a clear demarcation between work and play? Can work also be play? We are aware that it can be the other way round when we hear people say, 'This is more like hard work', while referring to a recreational pursuit and, conversely, we are familiar with people who say, 'I love my job. I would not call it work.' So we might conclude that when it comes to work and play, what is the difference and which is better? It is always difficult to generalise. We can only really individualise.

We are familiar with wildlife TV programmes when foresters, rangers, managers of animal parks and reserves are interviewed and asked about their role – a question that often provokes the inevitable emotive response: 'It's not a job. It's my hobby. I love it!' Many of us sit enviously watching these enthusiastic, highly-motivated people and realise that the prospect of our getting up the next day at 6:30am to catch the 7:22

along with two hundred fellow commuters is becoming more depressing – there must be more to life. If we acknowledge then that we all need an income and that it is best earned doing it our own way, then we might migrate our definition of work as the opportunity to perform our chosen activity for an habitable income return. This sounds better. It is less onerous than the traditional definition. 'Opportunity' and 'chosen activity' favour more user-friendly terminology and are much more motivational. It puts choice on your side of the fence. Within the traditional work environment the focus is primarily on what job we can get, rather than on what we would like to do.

However, if we are to travel along the 'want' rather than the 'should do' activity path, then we must expect a mixed reaction from our friends and peers. Imagine the following dialogue:

'What do you do?'
'I'm an orthopaedic surgeon.'
'That's a fascinating job.'
'No, not really – I spend most of my time performing

hip replacement operations. I find the work repetitive and boring and, as we have an ageing population, I am not looking forward to the prospect of doing more of the same job for the next 10 years. What do you do?'

'Well, for about four months of the year I am a ski instructor in Morzine, France and then for five months I canoe and give surfboarding instruction in Rock, Cornwall. For the rest of the year, I go travelling, exploring Africa or the Australian outback.'

'That sounds great, but what do you intend to do for a job when you settle down?'

'This is my job. I've been doing it for seven years now.'

You can imagine the reaction of the surgeon when, for a fleeting moment, they consider the unthinkable: 'I've always loved skiing and am quite good at it... It wouldn't take me long to get up to speed again and take the instructor's course... Must stop dreaming. Next patient, please!'

Yet, what is work to some is play to others. I realised this clearly when I joined a gym and discovered the experience of a torturous and extreme test of will power.

Whether it's on a treadmill, rowing machine, exercise bike or the cross-trainer, my goal is to complete the session as quickly as possible and get into the shower. I always envy the gym-goers who enjoy the activities and who monitor their fitness improvements by challenging themselves further during sessions. To me, efforts made at the gym are tantamount to hard work. To others, the workout corresponds to enjoyable, purposeful and satisfying recreation.

Deciding what is work and what is play is a decision that is entirely personal and never right or wrong. A visit to the gym is a good example; for me, it is an onerous duty and hard work. For others, it is a motivational experience and an enjoyable hobby.

Which factors motivate people to review career options?

From my experience, there is never a single factor. It can be a combination of events, personality and personal circumstances. When referring to events, I mean something unpredictable and outside your control. Your employer outsources your department to an overseas supplier; or your employer relocates and your role becomes redundant. Children may aspire to follow a parent's profession or decide that it is at the bottom of their list. A breakup of marriage or partnership may cause people to re-evaluate their work focus. It may be a planned change or a spontaneous one. There could also be a health issue, or an accident due to a sporting or recreational activity, such as skiing or perhaps something as simple as lifting that large box of books without keeping your back straight.

Is it an age thing?

Intrinsically, no. Age will not be an influencer as to whether you review your career options, but will be an influencer as to how you go about it.

If you substitute age for experience, then you could say that the more experience you have of life, the more definitive you will be in terms of what activities you enjoy and what sounds good in the short term but is not sustainable over a period.

The more experienced you are may mean that you are more cautious and the 'been there, done that' syndrome will apply. Family responsibilities or financial commitments will be factors that must be integrated into your choice of activity.

'I know that I dislike marmite but love Roquefort cheese. Yet, there was a time when I had not experienced either taste.'

'I'm fed up with the rat race'; 'Work is so boring' are common catalysts for change.

We know that, generally, as people get older they can inherit more financial obligations and their choice of gap year will be more confined than if they were a graduate living in rented accommodation without a mortgage. The big student loan that is the result of too many nights out is not considered as a debt, but rather something you will pay off in the future when you start a 'real job'.

We can conclude that having a gap year every year is not influenced or determined by age or, as we may euphemistically say, experience, but rather by the individual's circumstances, personality and events.

Is it an opt out or a cop out?

The question is only relevant to others and not to you. If you have decided to embark on what society regards as an unconventional career path, then that is society's judgement and not yours. Critical commentary of your ambitious intentions may be motivated by envy. We all know colleagues who constantly refer to their 'big plan' which never comes to fruition.

So, whether your family, friends or colleagues think that you are opting out or copping out, 'barking mad' or being very enterprising is not important and you should 'blaze your own trail', as we say. It can only be your decision.

Should you plan it or just go for it?

Now, if you decide to follow what society refers to as the 'opt out' route and it does not work out, you can always regroup and start again. I have deliberately not used the word 'failure' since new experiences can only be judged after the event. A new activity creates new events and new situations, which will be unpredictable in terms of outcome.

Today's society is short term and your choice of activity is a journey not a destination. But the do-it-now concept will generate different reactions dependent on your personality.

The Supporter will be the most nervous in terms of anticipating a negative outcome, and will need a lot of support and assurances from friends that they are doing the right thing and that risks are low. The Supporter will benefit from nominating a good friend as a mentor so that when they enter unknown territory, they can benefit from the encouragement and assurance that the party can offer.

The Supporter should keep reminding themselves of the task goals and not be immediately waylaid by negative and critical reactions. While embarking on a new activity, the Supporter will have a tendency to put off and frequently postpone the eventual starting point and may need strong encouragement (a big push) from their mentor.

The Influencer will engage naturally with the do-it-now concept. They enjoy initiative/enterprise and spontaneity and will not over plan. 'I'll find out when I get there.' 'Let's stop wasting time. We need to get going.' 'If we are short of things, we can buy them when we get there.' These are all typical 'off-the-cuff' remarks of an Influencer. Their lack of planning may mean that they are not fully aware that their destination is rather remote and does not offer the shopping facilities of their local supermarket. However, their positive, resourceful attitude will see them through.

The Creative will enjoy 'having a gap year every year'. Their inbuilt sense of adventure is based on their propensity for the new – new things to see, new experiences to enjoy. The Creative enjoys variety and momentum and will embrace change in that, by its nature, it presents new outcomes.

The Creative has a natural capacity to learn and needs this constant stimulus. Therefore, they should not look for an activity that is repetitive and predictable. The Creative is judgemental and highly imaginative and enjoys an environment where they can apply their unique skills. Applying originality, adapting a different approach and being unconventional are descriptors with which the Creative can identify. 'But it's never been done before,' will be interpreted as a challenge and not a fait accompli. The corollary, of course, is that an environment with onerous constraints in terms of politics or customs should be avoided at all costs. The Creative is pragmatic and will choose the most expedient time to embark on their new adventure.

The Analyst will plan and endeavour to anticipate all eventualities. Unlike the Influencer, they need to know exactly where they are going and how to get there, and will make lots of 'what if' provisions. So, if they are breaking a conventional mould and planning a dramatic career change, their attitude is not experimental but rather fully committal. They will persist if the first impressions or experiences are not up to their expectations. Their judgements will be rationally rather than emotionally based, and they will persevere to make things happen as they are not inclined to discard the many months of preparation and planning.

It is important that the Analyst does not adopt too prescriptive a mentality to their new ventures, otherwise when reality does not meet expectations, they could feel disorientated. Their adaptation to change and the unexpected takes time and is a slower process for them than, for example, the Influencer who regards change as synonymous with adventure.

When is the time right? We can see that different personalities will take a different approach. Knowing this, will help you to apply that knowledge contextually and prepare accordingly.

Let's round up

The general emphasis of *How to Have a Gap Year Every Year* is to give you, the reader, support, motivation and permission to think 'outside the square'. Too often, society is endeavouring to box us in with norms, traditions, protocols, parental expectations and peer pressures. This is a time when you can be self-indulgent without being selfish, unplanned without having a guilt complex and focused on a paid activity that you enjoy. Today's corporate societal targets are over concentrated on commercial goals, which crowd out the real values and benefits of enjoyment and ethics as goals that should be in the primary tier.

In my coaching and recruitment I see a major value shift. The credit crunch has fast-forwarded many people's concerns and doubts about the wisdom of Capitalism as the single-minded and unadulterated corporate role model. The credit crunch has exposed incompetence and what many people regarded as expert opinion to be no more than random guesswork. Thus, in this melee of facetious re-evaluations it is out with the structured career path, down with rampant competition and exploitation and in with opportunity life values and environmental stewardship.

The good news is that having a gap year every year will be a modern occurrence and now may be the time to throw off the shackles of convention, liberate your talents and skills and not grow old thinking: 'I wish…', 'If only…', 'I would love to have…'

So, have your gap year every year, review the personality descriptors and get as close as possible to doing what you enjoy and be paid for it. Treat it as a process not a sudden revelation. Be brave, be unconventional, be excited, be pioneering, be happy, and always, always **be you**.